Superflex® and Kool Q. Cumber to the Rescue!
Empower Your Thinkable® to Defeat Your Unthinkable®

WRITTEN BY:
Michelle Garcia Winner
AND THE SUPERFLEX CREATIVE TEAM

Superflex® and Kool Q. Cumber to the Rescue!

Written by Michelle Garcia Winner and the Superflex Creative Team

Copyright © 2018 Think Social Publishing, Inc.

All Rights Reserved except as noted herein.

This book may not be copied in its entirety, translated, or transferred to an alternative format for any reason without licensing from Think Social Publishing, Inc. (TSP). TSP grants permission to the owner of this product to use and/or distribute select pages of materials from it, "as is" or with owner-created modifications, in print or electronic format, only for *direct in-classroom/school/home or in-clinic use* with your own students/clients/children, and with the primary stakeholders in that individual's life, which includes the person's parents, treatment team members and related service providers.

All other reproduction/copying, adaptation, or sharing/distribution of content in this publication or on its CD (if applicable), through print or electronic means, requires written licensing from TSP.

All distribution or sharing of materials you create based on TSP works (educational worksheets, lesson plans, activities, games, etc.), via hard copy or posted electronically on the Internet, or on websites such as YouTube or TeachersPayTeachers.com, whether for free or a fee, is strictly prohibited.

Social Thinking, Superflex, The Unthinkables, The Thinkables, and We Thinkers! GPS are trademarks belonging to TSP.

Visit www.socialthinking.com to find detailed TERMS OF USE information and copyright/trademark FAQs covering using/adapting TSP concepts and materials, speaking on Social Thinking, Superflex or any other parts of our methodology, using the Social Thinking name, etc.

Illustrations by Deveo Media Studio

ISBN: 978-1-936943-48-7

Think Social Publishing, Inc.
404 Saratoga Avenue, Suite 200
Santa Clara, CA 95050
Tel: (408) 557-8595
Fax: (408) 557-8594

This book was printed and bound in the United States by Mighty Color Printing.

TSP is a sole source provider of Social Thinking products in the U.S.
Books may be purchased online at www.socialthinking.com

Recommended Teaching & Learning Pathway
for using the Superflex series and the *Superflex Curriculum*

3-Step Pathway for kids ages 5-10*

1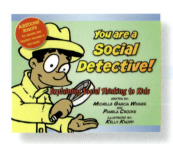

Use Social Detective first to introduce key Social Thinking concepts/Vocabulary to build social awareness.

2

After building social awareness and a social vocabulary, depending on the age of your student, introduce Superflex to teach strategies for self-regulation in a superhero-themed format.

3

Use Glassman (or any other Superflex books or games) AFTER teaching the Superflex Curriculum to take learning to a deeper level.

If you're working with kids ages 9-12

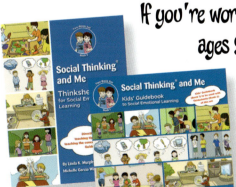

Social Thinking and Me is used BEFORE or alongside teaching the Superflex Curriculum.
This two-book set helps deepen students' understanding of core Social Thinking concepts and gives them lots of practice to build stronger social competencies.

Use Thinkable illustrated storybooks as companions to Unthinkable storybooks. Great tool for focusing on the positive powers in each of our brains.

*Some younger kids with social learning challenges may need more time building their Social Detective skills. Wait to start Superflex with them until around age 8.

Find articles and eLearning Modules, about teaching Superflex plus other books and teaching materials at
www.SocialThinking.com

To Social Town Citizens everywhere
who are learning to defeat their Unthinkables

While all children can benefit from the social emotional teaching that is at the foundation of Social Thinking, it was specifically designed to help promote social learning in children who have solid language and academic learning skills who also have social learning challenges (e.g. ASD, ADHD, twice exceptional, behavioral challenges, etc.). However, mainstream teachers now adopt our materials for use with students as they find them user-friendly for all.

Acknowledgments

Crafting stories and teaching materials is a group effort, with many minds working together. Our deepest thanks go out to the individuals who contributed to this project: Sandra Horwich, who developed the storyline and brought Kool Q. Cumber's personality and message to life; the folks at Deveo Media Studios, who transformed our ideas into colorful, visual illustrations (with an inordinate amount of patience through the many changes we made); and the Superflex Creative Team members. Our special thanks go to Ginny Thompson, who originally created and submitted Brakester to us. We found ourselves regularly asking this Power Pal to help us "throw on the brakes" to slow down and use our superflexible thinking to figure out what to do next. Ginny: as you look down from heaven, know that Social Town citizens everywhere remember your wonderful teaching powers!

Notes to Adults

In 2008, we released *Superflex®... A Superhero Social Thinking® Curriculum* to help children learn more about Social Thinking and self-regulation. Since that time children around the world (and the adults who teach or work with them) have embraced learning about their social strengths and challenges through Superflex and the 14 Unthinkable characters. They have created hundreds of new Unthinkable characters, and have turned the characters and concepts into classroom movies, plays, drawings, comic books, puppets and costumes.

In response to this overwhelming influx of support, in 2012 we released *Social Town Citizens Discover 82 New Unthinkables® for Superflex® to Outsmart!*, a compilation of 82 Unthinkables submitted by Social Town citizens. In that book we also introduced Superflex's five trusted friends, the Power Pals, and their very cool Five-Step Power Plan to help organize children's thinking so they could more effectively problem solve what's happening around them (the situation), the hidden rules, which Unthinkable was invading their brain, what strategy could be used to defeat the Unthinkable, and how to coach themselves through the process to regain or maintain self-regulation.

We also introduced the Thinkables® – characters who represent aspects of the superflexible brain power and positive efforts demonstrated by Social Town citizens in defeating their Unthinkables on an ongoing basis. Citizens could call on their Thinkable powers anytime, anyplace, to help them, and they did! Citizens loved the positive, empowering message the Thinkables represented. "I can defeat my Unthinkable! I can use my flexible thinking and strategies! I can do this!"

Each Unthinkable has a corresponding Thinkable character and each Thinkable character has its own special powers. In this book, we talk about **Kool Q. Cumber,** who helps citizens keep their cool (stay calm) so they can learn to self-regulate when problems occur. Kool Q. Cumber's powers help a citizen who is working to defeat the Unthinkable, Glassman, who causes people to have huge reactions to small problems.

Kool Q. Cumber to the Rescue! is a companion to the Superflex illustrated storybook, *Superflex® takes on Glassman and the Team of Unthinkables.* Children will see the same characters and settings in both books to help with understanding. Adults who are teaching/using the Superflex curriculum and concepts can use this Thinkable book in several ways:

1. To help children celebrate their ability to defeat Glassman when he appears
2. To teach about and illustrate how calling upon Kool Q. Cumber can help them learn to match the size of their reaction to the size of a problem
3. As a companion book to Glassman, to help children compare and contrast the inner workings of their brain in tackling everyday social challenges related to problem and reaction sizes
4. Use Kool Q. Cumber as a positive character substitute to shift attention in situations where students find it fun to only act out the negative powers of the Unthinkables. Focusing exclusively on the negative powers prevents students from learning how to defeat the Unthinkable!

Learn more about Superflex and the Superflex series of products at www.socialthinking.com

Welcome back to Social Town!

Social Town citizens are getting better and better at using their Superflex powers. And you know what? An awesome thing is happening - Thinkables are starting to show up more and more!

Thinkables help citizens use their superflexible strategies to make good choices and act in expected ways. This helps keep those pesky Unthinkables far away from Social Town!

This book is about the Thinkable Kool Q. Cumber, but there are others too!

Find other Thinkables on page 27.

The Thinkable
Kool Q. Cumber

I help citizens learn to "keep their cool" (be calm) when problems occur.

This helps keep the Unthinkable Glassman far far away!

The Unthinkable
Glassman

I make people have huge reactions to small problems.

The Thinkable Kool Q. Cumber (we call him Kool, for short!) helps Social Town citizens remember to stay calm when problems happen.

That way, citizens can stop and use their superflexible thinking to figure out the size of a problem. And, if a problem is only a small one, they can have only a small emotional reaction. That's expected!

This Thinkable was named after a saying that's more than 400 years old: "cool as a cucumber." When someone is described that way, it means the person works to control the size of their reaction, even when things feel frustrating.

Social Town Fun Fact

Even in hot weather, the inside of cucumbers is about 20 degrees cooler than the outside air! Now, that's cool!

A MONDAY MORNING IN SOCIAL TOWN

"Bark, we get to show our space projects in class today! I can't wait to show our Mars rover!"

Aiden heads off to school. Today the class will present science projects they've been working on. Aiden worked in a group with his friend Sam.

Sometimes Sam finds it hard to stay calm when problems happen. Glassman can invade his brain and he can have a big reaction to something that's really just a little problem.

Sam has been working hard to use the superflexible thinking strategies he learned at the Superflex Academy.
And Kool has been around to help him too!

STRATEGIES TO DEFEAT GLASSMAN

1. Ask myself "What is the size of the problem?"
2. Small problem = small reaction
3. Calm my body: breathe in, tighten up all my muscles, breath out and relax them
4. Call on my inner coach to use positive self-talk

Sam learned he can use his strategies to defeat Glassman no matter where or when he appeared. The more Sam practiced, the more his Kool Q. Cumber powers appeared to help him and the stronger they became!

Sam and Aiden are excited about Space Day. Let's hope things go smoothly... and if any problems happen Sam can call on his Kool Q. Cumber powers to help him stay calm and use his strategies.

Social Town Fun Fact

When Sam says "I'm chill" he means he's feeling calm and relaxed.

The students arrive at class with their projects for Space Day.

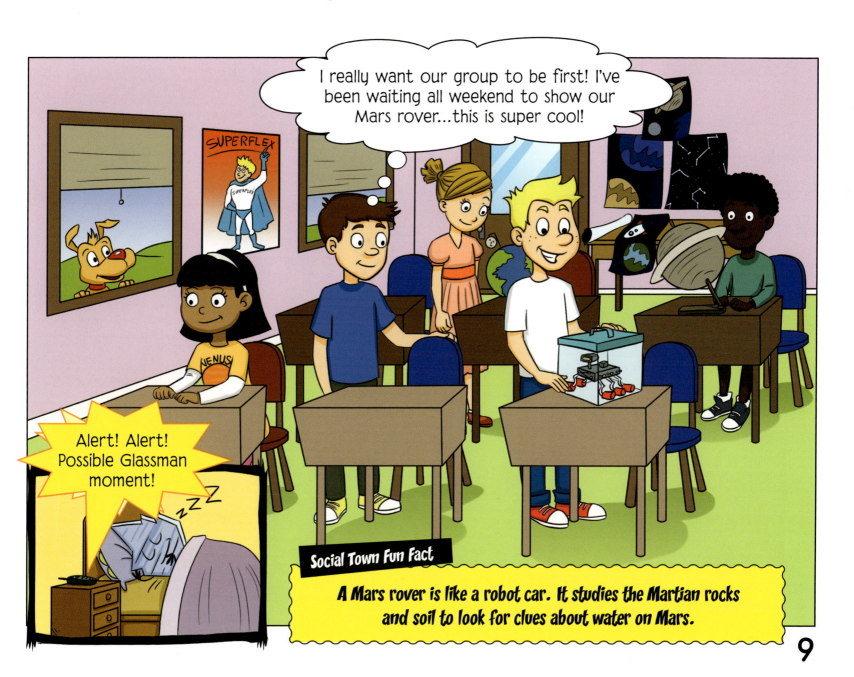

I really want our group to be first! I've been waiting all weekend to show our Mars rover...this is super cool!

Alert! Alert! Possible Glassman moment!

Social Town Fun Fact

A Mars rover is like a robot car. It studies the Martian rocks and soil to look for clues about water on Mars.

The students are excited for Space Day. Sam and Aiden are in a group that has Mars and Jupiter for their topic.

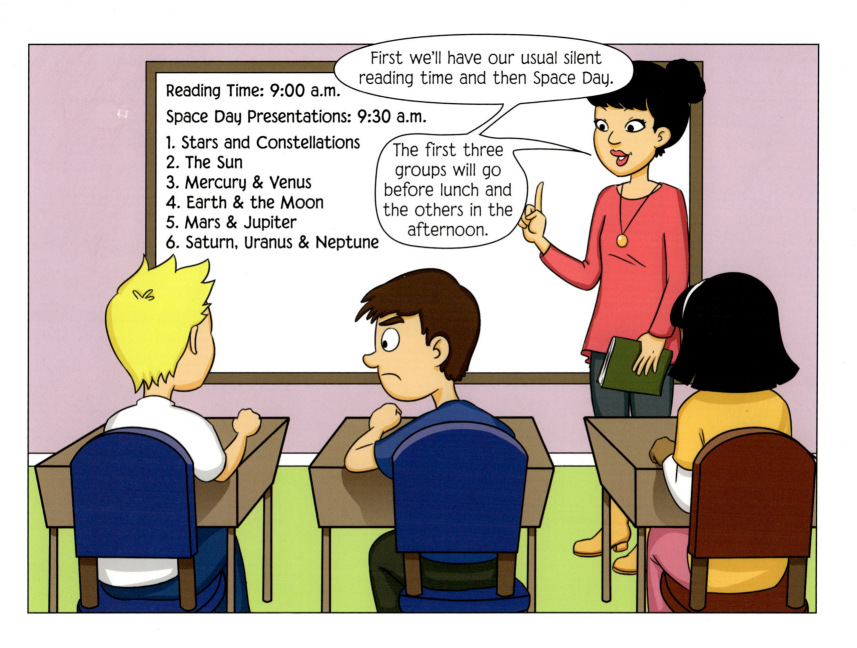

Ms. Kato goes over the day's schedule. The groups will present their projects in the order the planets are from the sun.

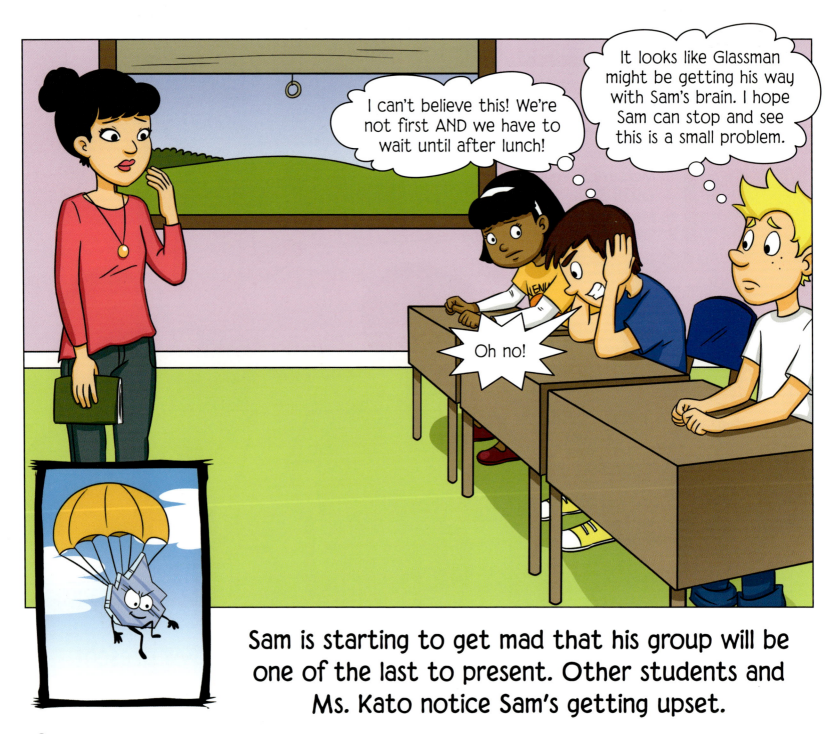

Superflex has five Power Pals who shared their very cool Five-Step Power Plan to help Social Town citizens defeat the sly Unthinkables.

Glassman is one of the most common Unthinkables. He tries to control citizens' brains so they think every tiny problem is huge, and then they have huge upset reactions over small problems.

- Decider helps us figure out which Unthinkable is trying to take over our brain.

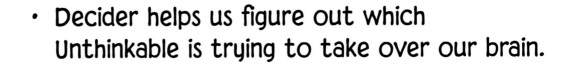
- Social Detective helps us look around at the situation and people in it for clues.

- Brakester helps us stop and think about the hidden rules.

- Flex Do Body helps us be flexible and choose a strategy to use.

- Cranium Coach helps us use positive self-talk.

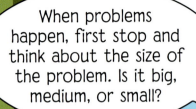

When problems happen, first stop and think about the size of the problem. Is it big, medium, or small?

Our superflexible thinking helps us notice that a problem isn't nearly as big as Glassman tries to make us think it is!

Losing a game or not getting to go to the restaurant you want are examples of small problems.

A strategy to calm your body is to make your muscles really tight as you breathe in. Relax your muscles as you breathe out.

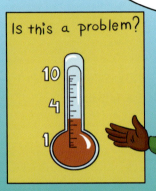

When we use our strategies we can figure out that if the problem is small, it's expected we show a small reaction. When we stay calm, the problem feels smaller and other problems won't make it worse. Kool Q. Cumber and his Thinkable buddies help us stay calm and flexible!

Ms. Kato asks students to put their books away and get ready for the Space Day presentations. Sam feels calmer after remembering strategies he can use.

Sam uses his superflexible thinking to figure out that waiting to present until the afternoon is no big deal. Thanks go to Kool Q. Cumber and Cranium Coach for helping Sam work through this.

In the afternoon, Aiden and Sam's group presented their Space Day project. There was no sign of Glassman. Kool Q. Cumber rocks!

Social Town Fun Fact

To "rock" is to do something that people think is awesome!

SUPERFLEX'S

Top Secret Tip Sheet
Other Unthinkables Kool Q. Cumber can help you defeat

Sometimes more than one Unthinkable can invade a person's brain – at the same time! The Thinkable Kool Q. Cumber can help you with some of these Unthinkables too!

The Unthinkable **Rock Brain** often appears around Glassman. Rock Brain makes people get stuck on their ideas, like when Sam wanted to present his group's project in the morning.

Another Unthinkable who can make a lot of trouble is **Worry Wall**, who makes people worry too much. Worry Wall got that name because when the power of worry sets in, it seems like people can't get away from it. Citizens feel like they're trapped by a big wall! Glassman often pairs up with Worry Wall to cause double the trouble! People worry about their small problems and get even more upset!

D.O.F., the Destroyer of Fun, makes people overly competitive! Glassman teams up with D.O.F. to make Social Town citizens get super upset if they lose a game! Kool Q. Cumber helps citizens chill, by realizing that it's better to play a game and lose than have no one to play with at all.

Many other Thinkables can help out too!

Remember to activate your Superflex by using strategies to defeat your Unthinkables, and make good choices that help you and the people around you feel calm and comfortable while you're together. When you practice doing that, the Thinkables' powers will appear!

SUPERFLEX and the Thinkables!

Stick-Withem - I help you keep your body with the group and your shoulders turned toward the group.

Tracker - I help you stay on the right track or topic the group is talking about.

I.O.F. - I help you use your positive thinking so you can cooperate and be flexible during sports and games.

Focus Tron - I help give you focusing powers so your brain can stay connected to what others are talking about or what you are doing.

Other-Side Sally - I help you remember that conversations are also about thinking about the other person or persons and finding out about them.

Space Respecter - I help you pay attention to and respect other people's personal space bubbles.

Posi Tina - I help you stay calm and positive to stay in control and defeat your worries.

Rex Flexinator - I help you be a flexible thinker so you don't get stuck on your own thoughts or plans.

Nice Bryce/Brice - I help you say nice, friendly words to others even if you don't feel like being friendly.

Socia-Lee Wonderer - I remind you to think about and use your social wonder questions so you can keep the other person interested during the conversation.

Kool Q. Comber - I help you stay calm (cool as a cucumber) when problems come up so you can see they are small and react with a small reaction.

Meditation Matt - I help you try to be calm throughout your day, so you can stop and think about making good choices.

Sonny Son - I help you see the good things in a day and feel pretty good about your life so you can always show your "sunny" side to others.

HumorUs - I help you know the right time and right place to use humor.

SocialThinking has so much to offer!

OUR MISSION

At Social Thinking, our mission is to help people develop social competencies to better connect with others and experience deeper well-being. We create unique treatment frameworks and strategies to help individuals develop their social thinking and related social skills to meet their academic, personal and professional social goals. These goals often include sharing space effectively with others, learning to work as part of a team, and developing relationships of all kinds: with family, friends, classmates, co-workers, romantic partners, etc.

ARTICLES
100+ free educational articles and treatment strategies

CONFERENCES, eLEARNING & CUSTOM TRAINING
Courses and embedded training for schools and organizations

PRODUCTS
Books, games, posters, music and more!

CLINICAL RESEARCH
Measuring the effectiveness of the Social Thinking Methodology

TREATMENT: CHILDREN & ADULTS
Clinical treatment, assessments, school consultations, etc.

CLINICAL TRAINING PROGRAM
Three-day intensive training for professionals

www.socialthinking.com